HELPERS
AND
HEALERS

ELENI KOHILAKIS

HELPERS AND HEALERS

iUniverse books may be ordered through booksellers or by contacting:

iUniverse
1663 Liberty Drive
Bloomington, IN 47403
www.iuniverse.com
844-349-9409

ISBN: 978-1-6632-1061-6 (sc)
ISBN: 978-1-6632-1060-9 (e)

Library of Congress Control Number: 2020919444

Print information available on the last page.

iUniverse rev. date: 10/27/2020

CONTENTS

AUTHOR BIO

Eleni Kohilakis is a graduate of Cornell University's College of Agriculture and Life Sciences with a major in Biological Sciences, a concentration in Human Nutrition, and a minor in Business for the Life Sciences. As someone who hopes to pursue a career in medicine, Eleni has become fascinated by the differences between health care systems of various nations. Eleni, the granddaughter of Greek immigrants, is a dual citizen of the U.S. and Greece. Her close ties to the immigrant population, her experiences interning at New York hospitals, and her visits to hospitals in Europe have inspired her to tell the stories of immigrants, both documented and undocumented, receiving medical care within the US healthcare system.

DEDICATION

To Yiayia Helen Tsourounakis and Papou Steve Kohilakis, who are no longer with us but who continue to shape the person I hope to become. Although I never had the chance to meet my Yiayia Helen, after whom I am named, I grew up hearing stories from my mom and grandpa and from the many strangers who were excited to share their memories of her. I know for certain that she is a woman I would have admired.

Both Helen and Steve immigrated to the United States from the island of Crete. I am amazed by their bravery and strength as they made lives for themselves in a country thousands of miles away from their true home—the island that Papou Steve called "the most beautiful place on Earth."

**Disclaimer: Most names contained in this book have been changed in order to maintain anonymity and privacy. **

PREFACE

This past summer, I had the opportunity to meet a fifteen-year-old undocumented immigrant from Guatemala who was stopped trying to cross the border between the US and Mexico in an attempt to reunite with her 21-year-old sister living in Mississippi. She was detained at the border with a concern of tuberculosis, after which she was sent to New York City. Although she was not traveling with any family, the current U.S. policy has separated migrant children from their parents, and many undocumented Central American immigrant children are brought from the US-Mexico border to a non-profit social service agency facility in NYC that provides foster care and other services under federal government grants. Upon her medical examination at the facility that suggested a TB (tuberculosis) infection, she was sent to the hospital where I was shadowing and doing research through a summer student program.

In the hospital, she was tested for tuberculosis with a PDD, and she presented with eosinophilia, which can be caused by parasites in the lung. Her X-ray showed calcifications that appeared to look like reactivation of the TB. Upon further examination, the X-ray was grossly concerning for primary tuberculosis, not reactivation. I was interested to learn that the Department of Health paid for her medications and that she would be able to go home with three negative TB smears.

Upon being faced with an individual directly affected by current policy changes, I was excited to learn about the logistics of her care. Immediately I asked the physician whom I was shadowing on rounds, "Why did they send her here? Who is paying for her care? Who do you consult for her important medical decisions?" I was surprised to learn that every test that was ordered had to be approved by our very own US Department of Health—the very people responsible for paying for her care. After she was given an official TB diagnosis, a waiting game began for this girl ... and for her family, who were spread across the Western Hemisphere.

The pain that I felt for this girl, all alone in a new country without a familiar face, hit rather close to home due to a very personal experience. I had never been forced to reflect on my experience within the US healthcare system, as my only time as a patient was for my yearly physicals with my pediatrician. It was not until my mother's breast cancer diagnosis in the spring semester of my freshman year of college that I really started paying attention. Accompanying her to her various appointments when I got home for the summer, I began to look at the way the hospital was functioning: the various controls that were in place to ensure patients were receiving the correct treatments or drugs, the teams of nurses, techs, and doctors responsible for each person's care, and so on.

I arrived back home after my final exams just in time for my mom's eight chemotherapy treatments—four weeks of AC (Adriamycin, a.k.a. "the red devil," and Cytoxan) and four weeks of Taxol. Although it was one of the most terrifying experiences of my life, I learned so much about the medical field by accompanying my mom to her appointments with her oncologist and her breast surgeon. I learned about the functions of steroids from the nurses, and about how oral supplements can interfere with the pathway of the chemotherapy drug from the nutritionist. I learned about the importance of bedside manner. I became an expert in cooling caps, which are used to freeze the hair follicles before, during, and after treatment to stop the chemotherapy from burning away the hair follicles in an attempt to save the patient's hair. I also learned about cooling gloves and boots, which are used to freeze the toes and fingertips to prevent the permanent tingling that results from damage to nerve endings, known as neuropathy, which is a symptom of the Taxol drug. From the breast surgeon I learned about the healing of wounds, how to look out for infection, and how it is possible to graft the tissue from one's abdomen to one's breast and reattach each of the blood vessels (also known as anastomosis). This procedure, termed a DIEP (deep inferior epigastric perforators) flap reconstruction, is a long and grueling surgery that takes around eight hours in the operating room. At each appointment we went to, the doctors were speaking directly to me because they could tell how engrossed I was in all the information. They entrusted me to make sure that I looked after my mom when we were home—to change her bandages, to check her scabs, to apply numbing cream to her port (where her veins were accessed during chemotherapy), to remind her to take her steroids, to make her an Epsom salt bath, to remind her not to touch her hair, to make sure she didn't sleep on her stomach… It was so much information to take in—far too much for my mom to remember as she was combating this horrible disease.

Our experience at the treatment center was not always delightful. The nurses were rude at times. Other times we would have to wait for hours to be taken into the room, or the team would not know how to use the scalp cooling machine (which had recently been implemented at the hospital). New problems would arise every visit, but the general procedure was always the same: do a blood draw, have it checked by the lab, start getting hydration and pre-meds (a battery of medications including steroids, anti-nausea medication, a saline solution, and Benadryl), get the chemo, get post-hydration. Standard operating procedure. But during my mom's third treatment, the nurse hooked up the Cytoxan to her IV as the first step. My mother had not received any of her pre-meds yet and had also not received the Adriamycin, which MUST be given before the Cytoxan. As soon as I recognized this error, I confronted the nurse and asked her why she hadn't given any of the other medication, to which she responded, "It's fine, it doesn't matter. The doctor ordered it this way." I asked her to please double-check the protocols as to what medications my mother had received last time and in what order. I explained to her that this was not correct. At first, she completely shut me down. Frankly, she was irritated that I, a teenager, was telling her how to do her job. I stood my ground because my mother's life was in this woman's hands and, in my opinion, this nurse was simply being careless. She argued with me that the doctor hadn't ordered those medications from the pharmacy this time, but I was not going to back down. I found the head nurse coordinator and explained the situation to her. Finally, after the head nurse coordinator came over, the nurse who had made the error admitted that I was right and thanked me for saying something.

There were other times during the summer when I had to confront authority figures at the hospital, such as when my mom's cooling cap was not kept on her head long enough following the chemotherapy treatment. I learned that you need to be your own best advocate and do your own research. I was in a position where I needed to press the oncologist for answers to my questions: Is it better to do the dose-dense Taxol over four weeks, or the 12-week Taxol regimen? How would we check that the cancer was cleared from the lymph nodes if it never came up on her original PET scan? How would we ensure that the chemotherapy had treated the two spots that were found on her lungs? Where would she receive the radiation treatment since all her original breast tissue had been removed?

Following this experience, I became rather cynical about the whole healthcare system. It seemed taken for granted that careless errors are bound to happen—unless you are able to advocate for yourself or are fortunate enough to have someone else who is able to speak on your behalf. I began to think about all the elderly people in the chemo infusion center who have no one to question the doctors like I was able to do for my mom. Thinking about all the people who need an advocate is what ultimately drew me to study medicine, as I want to be the person to stand up for those people.

I can't help but wonder: if I wasn't there for my mom, who would have challenged those individuals on their mistakes? Who would have ensured my mom was receiving the proper treatment? The undocumented Guatemalan girl with tuberculosis had no one by her side except a social worker she had just met.

This experience made me recognize the need to have an advocate during medical treatments, something which is certainly lacking from the experiences of undocumented immigrants who have been separated from their families and sent thousands of miles away to be treated, or even documented immigrants that have no idea what to expect when receiving care in a new country where they face numerous unforeseen obstacles.

In this book, I have gathered many similar stories to give us outsiders the chance to hear firsthand about these individuals' experiences. It is my hope that we can empathize with them in their times of pain and sorrow, and educate ourselves so that we may shape the future of medicine.

CHAPTER 1

BACKGROUND

Before I begin, I would like to address some basic facts about immigration policy in the US. The United States immigration system is based on three principles: (1) reunification of families, (2) admitting immigrants with skills that are valuable to the US economy, and (3) protecting persons fleeing persecution and for other humanitarian reasons.

To obtain a Lawful Permanent Residency status, typically known as individuals who have a "green card," an individual must pay a $1,070 filing fee and have their fingerprints entered into a national database. To become eligible to apply for US citizenship, an individual must have had lawful permanent residency status for at least five years (or three years if obtained LPR status through a spouse who is a US citizen or through the Violence Against Women Act), which involves a $680 filing fee also including fingerprints. Undocumented immigrants are individuals who have lost permission to remain in the US or who entered the US without permission.

There is no numerical limit for immediate relatives of US citizens, including spouses, unmarried minor children, and parents of US citizens. Under the family preference system, there are a limited number of visas available for adult children and siblings of US citizens, and spouses and unmarried children of lawful permanent residents. A United States citizen or Lawful Permanent Resident must sponsor a petition for their relative, establish the legitimacy of their relationship, meet the minimum income requirements, and sign an affidavit of support. The path to obtain lawful permanent residency may range from months to decades.

Temporary workers may qualify for nonimmigrant visas. More than 20 types of temporary work visas exist, such as for special occupations (e.g., nursing and agriculture), for intra-company transfers, for athletes, for entertainers and skilled performers, and for religious workers. The majority of available visas are for highly skilled workers who are sponsored by a specific employer.

The Affordable Care Act includes strong privacy protections for personally identifiable information, which is designed to encourage the participation of eligible individuals in mixed-status immigrant families. In other words, if an individual is to apply for health insurance but has an undocumented family member, they will be protected by the Affordable Care Act. Agencies can only collect, use, and disclose information that is necessary for enrollment in health coverage. The US Department of Homeland Security (DHS) or US Immigration and Customs Enforcement (ICE) has issued guidance that information about applicants and their households obtained for health insurance eligibility will not be used for civil immigration enforcement purposes.

Social security numbers are generally required for Medicaid applicants. However, coverage cannot be denied or delayed pending issuance or verification of a social security number. In addition, Medicaid agencies must help individuals apply for a social security number if they are eligible and don't have one, or if they don't know their social security number.[1]

The Personal Responsibility and Work Opportunity Reconciliation Act, a 1996 federal welfare reform law, prevented immigrants from being eligible for Medicaid; as a result, individuals who entered the United States after August 1996 were unable to receive medical coverage (except in emergencies) for their first five years within the United States. Prior to the passing of this law, legally admitted immigrants had the same access to Medicaid as did US citizens.

Nearly one-fifth of the children in the United States are immigrants or are the US-born children of immigrants.[2] In 2010, there were about 40 million foreign-born individuals living in the United States. It is predicted that by 2050 there will be approximately 83 million foreign-born people in the United States if present trends continue. This means that in the next thirty years the number of immigrants living in the United States will double in size.[3]

CHAPTER 2

HELEN

Being of Greek descent, my family often travels to Greece to visit our relatives. Driving to mountain villages with a population of 30, all with the same last name and men with the same curly mustache, triggered a realization in me. Without seeing the way these people lived with my own eyes, I would never have truly understood. Looking out the window during the taxi ride from the airport to the city of Xania, it amazed me how different my life was from the individuals whom we passed by. The glass separated us, but as I glimpsed into their world, a world so different from my own, I began to see. I saw their hardships, their pain, their loss, their sense of faith, their pride, and their love for a country that gives them a home. But it was not until I ventured up to the mountains and saw the men picking olives from the acres of orchards that I began to see the importance of tradition and culture. I learned that these men had taken on the occupations of their fathers, and their fathers' fathers. Not until we travel to places outside our own home do we truly begin to understand that there is more to the human story than what can be found in the short blurb on the back cover.

Crete is the big island south of the Greek mainland. It was home to both my maternal and paternal ancestors. This island made considerable contributions to Greek history and culture as a whole, but Cretans also pride themselves on their own local traditions. Crete is perhaps most famous for being the center of the ancient Minoan civilization. Additionally, Cretan resistance to German occupation during the Second World War was important in slowing down Hitler's advance in the region, something which Cretans still speak about to this day.

Coming from a poor Greek family living up in the mountains in the small, remote village of Tsourounouia, eight-year-old Helen Tsourounakis had no idea what life in the United States would hold. She was the eldest child, and she took the ship over to America with her mother and sisters at a time when the crew supposedly threw sickly immigrants overboard. Her mother, Anna, hid Helen's twin sisters, Evelyn and Catherine, just sixth months old, in a shoebox because they were both born prematurely. Anna had her appendix taken out when she was six months pregnant, and the twins were delivered at that time. On the boat, the Greeks, including the Tsourounakis family, were picked on and called "Greece balls." Eventually arriving in New York City by way of Ellis Island, the Tsourounakis family set out to begin their new lives in America.

Upon entering the United States, Helen's family was too poor to be able to support all their children. Because she was the eldest, Helen was sent to an orphanage called St. Basil's Academy in upstate New York, run by the Greek Orthodox Archdiocese of America. About 10 years after arriving in the states, Helen, described as a 4'11" female with fair complexion, hazel eyes, and brown hair, became a citizen on November 4, 1954, at the age of 16. Her certificate of citizenship states that she resided at 501 West 29th Street, New York City, NY. Years after arriving she met my grandfather, a child of Greek immigrants, who had climbed the ranks from mail boy to dishwasher to the general manager of a country club in Westchester, NY.

Following some general discomfort that was ignored, Helen eventually went to seek out medical attention. Helen was diagnosed with ovarian cancer in 1977 at the age of thirty-nine. Thankfully, she had access to medical insurance through her husband's job.

Ovarian cancer is a cancer that originates in the ovaries, the parts of the female reproductive system that produce eggs. This type of cancer is particularly deadly due to the fact that it goes largely undetected until it spreads up to the pelvis and abdomen, at which point it becomes very difficult to treat. Symptoms of ovarian cancer are also mistaken for common ailments, which leads to its late detection. Symptoms may include weight loss, abdominal bloating or swelling, discomfort, a frequent need to urinate, and constipation. Individuals with a family history of breast and ovarian cancer are at a much higher risk.

Today, there are various treatment options for ovarian cancer. Local treatments, which treat the tumor without affecting the rest of the body, include both surgery and radiation therapy. Systemic therapies are characterized by reaching cancer cells almost anywhere in the body. These therapies can be ingested orally or may enter intravenously. Systemic treatments include chemotherapy, hormone therapy, and targeted therapy. The treatment plan ultimately chosen by the physician and the patient is based on the type of ovarian cancer, how far it has spread, and other important considerations. Today, most women undergo surgery to remove the tumor and then receive some other type of additional treatment either before or after the surgery.[4]

Following her diagnosis, Helen received treatment at Memorial Sloan Kettering, a cancer treatment center and research institution at the forefront of their field, located in New York City. Helen received chemotherapy as the primary method of treatment, as well as various holistic treatment approaches. Because of the thick Greek hair she inherited from her parents, Helen never lost her locks during treatment.

Helen surpassed the limited number of years that her oncologist had originally given as her prognosis. The cancer seemed to abate for a period of time, but she eventually relapsed and wound up back in the hospital. Helen passed away at the age of 41 in 1980, leaving behind her thirteen-year-old daughter, her eight-year-old son, and her husband.

As a second-generation Greek-American, my Greek heritage is an incredibly large part of my identity. In traveling to our home in Greece each summer to visit relatives and immerse myself in the culture of our ancestors, I began to evaluate the Greek health care system following my experiences back home on American soil. I couldn't help but listen when I heard my relatives talking about promising Greek physicians leaving to go to America as a result of the low pay and poor working conditions that many young doctors face in Greece.

Although Helen left Greece before she was unable to fully experience the Greek health care system on a personal level, my discussions with friends and relatives who have received medical attention back in Greece within the past few years allows me to paint a decently clear image of how their experience would compare to a US hospital.

Currently, Greece has a surplus of at least 20,000 specialized doctors even though there is an evident lack of general practitioners. The number of doctors in Greece has risen disproportionately to Greece's population of 10.7 million people. A substantial percentage of these physicians are either unemployed or underemployed, with the number reaching as high as 28% in Athens, the capital. Because of this, 17,500 Greek doctors have left the country to find work. Despite the surplus of doctors, the ongoing financial crisis has left the Greek National Health System with physician shortages, with an estimated 6,000 vacant posts for doctors at Greek public hospitals. A study conducted by the Greek Health Ministry and the World Health Organization found that Greece needs another 4,350 family doctors in order to be on par with the European Union average of around 8,140 general practitioners in the EU member states.[5]

Despite these shortcomings of the Greek system, it exhibits certain qualities that have been lost in the US as a result of an economically driven attempt to lower cost and increase access while possibly diminishing quality. Although the Greek system may be a bit archaic, it is still a more personalized system as a result of its failure to evolve into what is called "Big Medicine," a term coined by Atul Gawande that critiques the takeover of hospitals and medicine by big business. Greece offers a look at a system that is relatively untouched by big business, exhibiting both the pros and cons of such a system.

The Greek healthcare system is built upon the coexistence of a National Health System, social insurance, and a voluntary private healthcare system. The National Health System provides universal coverage to the population. Meanwhile, the entire population is covered by social insurance funds and 15% of the population also has complementary voluntary health insurance coverage. The complementary health insurance, as well as out-of-pocket payments, fund a large private healthcare market. [6]

Many European countries have documented a loss of young physicians to other countries, including the United States. For example, in response to many young physicians leaving Hungary to practice elsewhere, the Hungarian government has begun to offer higher wages in order to entice these individuals to stay in their native country. The quality of physicians, available resources, and cultural attitudes toward medical care all have an influence on the experience of the patient in the health-care setting.

CHAPTER 3

ANA

Ana worked as a housekeeper in the home of a family located on Long Island, NY. She came from Honduras in search of income to send back home. Ana was diagnosed with vaginal melanoma, but as an undocumented immigrant, she was unable to qualify for Medicaid within the United States. Thankfully, the father in the family who employed her was a cardiologist and the mother was a retired nurse. Both of them were able to give her medical guidance about how to obtain treatment for her cancer. Ana soon took advantage of all the treatment that was available to her.

Ana began working for the family in May 2003, when their youngest daughter was just six weeks old. Ana was 44 years old and had come to American two years prior. Upon arriving in the US, Ana tried for years to become a citizen, working with lawyers and paying a lot of money out of her own pocket with no success.

She had a grown son who was married with two children, as well as a mother and a few siblings who remained in Honduras. She was divorced before she came to America. Ana was working to send money back to Honduras, and she was also supporting family here in the US; her son was an ironworker who was not employed consistently and one of her grandchildren had special needs. Any time the family she worked for got rid of old clothes and other items to donate to charity, Ana would send them back to Honduras.

Ana had a brother, sister-in-law, and niece in Brooklyn; a sister in Texas; and another sister in Mexico. In the summer of 2016, Ana's sister from Mexico came to stay with her. The sister expressed her concerns, saying that she was worried that Ana wasn't telling her the full story about her health. Ana's sister spent four weeks with her in the United States, working with Ana and accompanying Ana to all her appointments.

Ana was described as "a very sweet woman with the warmest smile." She treated the family she worked for like her own and they treated her the same. If Ana wasn't going to her brother's house in Brooklyn for a holiday, she spent it with her adopted family. When they would travel, Ana would stay at their house and take care of their dog, who adored her.

Ana was a very smart woman who was extremely diligent about her health. She was a hard worker and never asked anyone for a handout. She worked harder than was expected of her. She took great pride in her work, always responding "No problema!" to any task asked of her.

Besides being a hard-worker, she had a creative side. She had a great eye for decorating and for colors. She loved to help decorate for the holidays and would always ask to set the dining room table when guests were coming over. She would iron the tablecloth, take out the china and silver, and make a beautiful table. It made her so happy.

Ana was also an undocumented immigrant who was unable to qualify for Medicaid. Due to this barrier to access, she was thankful enough to find a local clinic that was able to provide her with care. She had established a relationship with the clinic in 2003, and she paid her bills on a sliding scale that the hospital determined. She was extremely conscientious, going for routine mammograms, colonoscopies, and yearly checkups. In the late spring of 2015, she was experiencing some vaginal discomfort. Upon going to the doctor, she was told that it was related to menopause. When her discomfort continued, she went back to the doctor in August of the same year and was diagnosed with vaginal melanoma. There was a lymph node involved in her groin.

Vaginal melanoma is a rare but aggressive malignancy that normally affects women in their 6th and 7th decade of life, appearing as a dark node or spindle.[7] In general, melanoma is a malignant tumor, which originates in melanocytes, the cells which produce the pigment melanin. Melanomas usually appear black or brown and are highly metastatic. They are normally characterized by asymmetry, border irregularity, dark color, a diameter larger than 6 mm, and an evolving nature. Vaginal melanomas are infrequently cured, and the involvement of Ana's lymph node at diagnosis was strongly predictive of a poor prognosis. The optimal treatment approach for patients with vaginal melanoma remains unclear, but surgery is the primary treatment for cutaneous melanomas, followed by radiotherapy used in the adjuvant setting.[8]

Although having a close relationship with the mother and father of the family she worked for, who were both involved in the health care industry, was indeed helpful, Ana conducted a lot of research on the internet about her diagnosis and treatment, and she was primarily responsible for educating herself. Thankfully, she faced no language barrier upon attending her appointments, as her doctors were bilingual and able to communicate with her in her native tongue.

Her doctors informed her that her melanoma could be treated with immunotherapy. The American Cancer Society defines immunotherapy as a treatment that uses parts of a person's immune system to fight disease. This can be done by stimulating one's immune system to attack cancer cells or by introducing man-made immune system proteins. Immunotherapy is the preferred treatment for certain cancers,[9] and so Ana was placed on a very expensive treatment protocol that was very effective. Ana also had to go through radiation treatment, which is used to kill cancer cells and shrink tumors with high doses of radiation. The hospital provided transportation back and forth for her doctor visits and for her radiation treatments. She had to pay $5.00 for the 30-minute door-to-door service.

As immigrants in a foreign country, many individuals often find themselves alone with no one to relate to. Thankfully, Ana found a friend in the family's carpenter who had worked on their house for years. John was fluent in Spanish, and when Ana was first diagnosed, John took her to the doctors for emotional support. He got her a binder and had her write everything down that the doctors told her. The mother of the household that Ana worked for accompanied her to the appointment when the doctor explained the treatment protocols. The immunotherapy ultimately gave Ana an additional two years of life after being diagnosed with this fatal disease.

At the end of June 2017, Ana was complaining that her shoulder was bothering her and she thought that she had pulled a muscle. A week had passed, and the family was on vacation; when they returned, they found out that Ana was in the hospital. The family did not know at the time, but the cancer had spread and was responsible for the pain in Ana's shoulder. That summer she spent weeks in the hospital. She barely disclosed any information to the family—whether she did it because she wanted to keep it private or because she didn't accept her fate is still unknown. In August, she found out that the cancer had spread and the treatments were no longer working. Two days later, Ana decided to leave for Honduras.

Ana became part of her new family, so when she was given only a few weeks to live, she couldn't face telling them. They paid for her flight home and didn't hear from her after that. In September 2017, Ana's niece informed them that Ana had passed away.

Although Ana was an undocumented immigrant, the individuals surrounding her gave her the support and guidance that she needed in order to battle her fate for two additional years compared to what was expected from her already rare diagnosis.

CHAPTER 4

HILDA

Hilda was a young, undocumented immigrant with two little boys. She suffered from End Stage Renal Disease (ESRD), also known as kidney failure. The typical treatment for ESRD involved dialysis three times per week, but because Hilda was undocumented and without insurance, the medical coverage available in Colorado only provided her with dialysis once a week and only when she was critically ill. Hilda received treatment at the hospital associated with UC Boulder.

Within Colorado, there are 538,000 foreign-born individuals out of 4.8 million total people. In Colorado, ten percent of the population are immigrants, with fifty-three percent coming from Latin America, including South America, Central America, Mexico, and the Caribbean. Forty-nine percent of immigrants have been in the United States longer than fifteen years, and twenty-three percent of all children in Colorado have at least one foreign-born parent. Forty-seven percent of foreign-born people in Colorado (239,000 people) are "Limited English Proficient" and speak English less than "very well." Seventeen percent of all people in Colorado speak a language other than English at home. Spanish is the most common language spoken by individuals who classify as "Limited English Proficient," with 226,000 speakers.

When observing the uninsured rates by race and ethnicity within Colorado, Hispanics have the highest uninsured rate. There have been great reductions in the number of individuals that are uninsured; however, disparities in coverage continue to exist. Hispanics make up 20.7% of all Coloradans but 37.6% of uninsured Coloradans, a statistic that clearly illustrates their lack of access to care when compared to other ethnic groups.[10] Immigrants in Colorado have varying eligibility for health coverage programs. Those eligible for Medicaid and CHP+ include "qualified" immigrants who entered before August 22, 1996, immigrants who reach the end of the five year waiting period (i.e., Lawful Permanent Residency/green card holders), immigrants exempt from the 5-year waiting period (e.g., refugees, asylees, Cuban/ Haitian entrants, trafficking victims, veteran families, etc.), "lawfully present" pregnant women and "lawfully present" children, and certain "lawfully present" seniors who are receiving the cash benefit under Colorado's Old Age Pension (OAP).

Refugees and asylees are two groups of individuals who cannot return to their home country because of a "well-founded fear of persecution" due to race, membership in a social group, political opinion, religion, or national origin. A refugee must apply for admission from outside the US and outside their home country. There is a numerical ceiling set each year by the President in consultation with Congress regarding the number of refugees. Refugees may apply to become lawful permanent residents after one year. Asylees are persons already in the US who were persecuted or fear persecution upon their return. They must apply within one year of arriving in the United States. There is no numerical limit for the number of asylees, and they may apply to become lawful permanent residents one year after receiving asylum. Trafficking survivors include individuals who were subject to sex trafficking, forced or fraudulent recruitment, harboring, transport, involuntary servitude, peonage, debt bondage, or slavery.

Immigrants eligible for "Connect for Health Colorado" include "lawfully present" immigrants ineligible for Medicaid or CHP+, including those with incomes under 100% of the federal poverty level who are ineligible for Medicaid/CHP+ based on immigration status. Lawfully present immigrants include qualified immigrants and other additional immigrants. Qualified immigrants include Lawful Permanent Residents, refugees, asylees, Cuban/ Haitian entrants, individuals paroled into the US, conditional entrants, battered spouse, child, and parent, trafficking survivors and his/ her spouse, child, sibling, or parent, and individuals withholding of deportation or withholding of removal. Other lawfully present immigrants include those granted relief under the Convention Against Torture, those with Temporary Protected Status, those with Deferred Enforced Departure, individuals with nonimmigrant status (includes worker visas, student visas, etc.), those included in the administrative order staying removal issued by the department of homeland security, and lawful temporary residents.

Undocumented immigrants are ineligible for Medicaid/CHP+ (except Emergency Medicaid) and ineligible to purchase qualified health plans in the individual marketplaces, even at full price. They can purchase private coverage outside the marketplace or through an employer, and they can apply for health insurance for eligible family members and be part of the household of eligible family members. Undocumented individuals are exempt from the individual mandate created under the Affordable Care Act as "exempt non-citizens," along with individuals who are "non-resident aliens" under current tax law. The individual mandate is a fine, in the form of a tax, that the government has instituted in order to get more people to sign up for health insurance. However, in 2019 the individual mandate will be removed. If these individuals are applying for premium tax credits on behalf of eligible family members, they must file a tax return. If these individuals are not eligible for a social security number, they may file a tax return using an individual taxpayer identification number.[11]

Hilda came to the United States from Mexico in her late teens and worked as a housekeeper in a hotel. As a young adult, Hilda had no medical problems. Because she came to the US in her late teens, she likely never saw a clinician in Mexico, as she developed kidney disease after moving to the US.

Hilda had two sisters in Colorado, but they were estranged. She had a home and some money once she settled in the US, but after she was diagnosed with kidney failure, her father was deported from the US by ICE, leaving her and her two boys homeless. She had no family or friends that she could stay with. The physicians overseeing her care at the UC Boulder Hospital gathered a multidisciplinary group to find her housing and were able to do so through a local shelter. Hilda had a little motel room with a kitchen and two bedrooms where she lived for free for the last year-and-a-half of her life. Hilda had no support system except for her health care providers.

Hilda was only able to receive care under Emergency Medicaid. Emergency Medicaid is available to undocumented immigrants who meet the eligibility requirements for Medicaid regardless of their immigration status. Coverage extends only to specific emergencies, including coverage of labor and delivery and 60 days post-partum care. Hilda had two to three cardiac arrests from waiting to receive dialysis only when she was in a state of emergency, and after a while, she decided that she couldn't keep "almost dying" given the emotional distress it was causing her children. The physician that treated Hilda described her as "one of the strongest people she has ever met." Hilda loved her boys more than anything else in the world and decided that she wanted to stop receiving dialysis so that her boys could live a normal life.

Just before Hilda passed away, she asked Dr. Cervantes, the primary physician that cared for her, to work with the Mexican consulate so that she could see her family one last time. They helped her get a visa and she flew home. Unfortunately, even at home she was unable to get the three-times-per-week dialysis treatment that she needed. Hilda was offered dialysis at a cost of $100 per session, and upon moving back to Mexico, she purchased two sessions;

however, her ultimate goal of returning home was to die. She did not want to be dependent on dialysis any longer and did not want her boys to continue to worry about the status of her health.

Dr. Cervantes explained that as clinicians, it is hard to see patients die because they are being provided with suboptimal care. No matter how much they like the patient and feel an attachment to them, it is not within the power of the physician to give the patient access to certain medications and procedures due to the various health insurance regulations within each state.

Health systems around the world have struggled with combatting the increasing rates of incidence and prevalence of chronic kidney disease (CKD). This battle has proven harder and even more significant for undeveloped countries. In Mexico, human and economic resources are insufficient for treatment despite the fact that the prevalence of chronic kidney disease is comparable to that in highly developed nations. Mexico has proposed various measures to improve their high mortality rates and noncompliance with established standards and guidelines, including programs for the prevention of obesity, diabetes, and hypertension; however, Mexico is still lagging behind the US in terms of treatment for this crippling condition.[12]

Hilda's decision to stop treatment because the stress was too much for her and her two young children is extremely upsetting. Her decision is understandable given that her heart stopped more than once and her ribs were fractured from receiving CPR, but it is unfair that she had to make such a decision in the first place. The risk of death for someone receiving dialysis only on an emergency basis is 14 times higher than someone getting standard care. There are an estimated 6,500 undocumented immigrants in the United States with End Stage Kidney Disease, and many are barred from Medicare or Medicaid. Treatment of these individuals varies widely from state to state, and in many places the situation is the same as in Colorado. Because of the difficulties of receiving care, individuals often have to wait for the onset of an emergency, such as dangerously high potassium levels, in order to receive dialysis. In some instances, patients consume large amounts of orange juice to reach high ion levels (which can be harmful to their health) in order to be able to qualify for emergency treatment.

These avoidable emergencies strain hospital resources by having immigrants take up space in emergency departments when they could be receiving dialysis outside of the hospital in dedicated clinics. In addition, Baylor College of Medicine found that emergency-only dialysis costs nearly four times as much as standard dialysis. An article published in the Journal of Clinical Nephrology found that at an Indianapolis hospital the state was paying significantly more for emergency-only dialysis than it did for more routine care.[13]

Arizona, New York, Washington, and several other states have modified their emergency Medicaid programs to include standard dialysis for undocumented immigrants. Had this been the case in Colorado, Hilda would still be alive today.

CHAPTER 5

NELSON

Nelson is a 49-year-old immigrant facing deportation back to Honduras. He entered the country illegally but has lived in Stamford, CT, for 30 years. He is married to a US citizen and has three children who were all born in the United States. He has Type 2 diabetes, high blood pressure, and renal failure, which requires him to receive dialysis every two days (about three or four times a week). Nelson receives private health insurance through his wife, and he is on track to receive a scheduled kidney transplant from his friend. However, his deportation would get in the way of these plans.

There are two types of treatment for kidney failure: dialysis or transplant. The only permanent solution to his health problems would be a kidney transplant, as his dependence on dialysis is extremely debilitating. A kidney transplant is a surgical procedure in which a healthy kidney from a live or deceased donor is placed into a person whose kidneys no longer function properly. The kidneys function to remove wastes and extra water from the blood in order to form urine. The excretory system, of which the kidneys are a major player, is responsible for the elimination of wastes produced by homeostasis. Homeostasis is the body's tendency to maintain levels at a set point through the use of physiological processes.

When an individual is in need of a kidney transplant, they are typically "added to the transplant list" by a transplant hospital. This is the UNOS (United Network for Organ Sharing) computer system. When a deceased organ donor is identified, UNOS's computer system generates a ranked list of transplant candidates based on a variety of criteria including blood type, tissue type, medical urgency, waiting time, expected benefit, geography, etc. A healthy person can become a living donor on the UNOS list by donating a kidney, or a part of the liver, lung, intestine, blood, or bone marrow. In the case of Nelson, he was not placed on a UNOS list, as he had made arrangements with a private donor.

Type 2 diabetes, another condition that Nelson has, was once known as adult-onset or noninsulin-dependent diabetes. It is a chronic condition that affects the metabolization of glucose, a sugar that is the body's primary source of energy. Individuals with Type 2 diabetes either resist the effects of insulin, a hormone released by the pancreas in response to high blood sugar that regulates the movement of glucose into cells, or don't produce enough insulin to maintain a normal glucose level. There is no cure for Type 2 diabetes, but the condition can be managed by eating well, exercising, and maintaining a healthy weight. If diet and exercise aren't enough to manage your blood sugar, individuals also may need diabetes medications or insulin therapy. The primary treatment for Type 1 Diabetes, which is an autoimmune disorder in which the beta cells of the pancreas do not produce insulin, is typically insulin. In Type 2 diabetes patients, insulin is not a needed treatment at first, and is only needed after their own endogenous insulin production slows down.

Potential complications of diabetes include kidney damage, also known as nephropathy. Diabetes can damage the kidney's filtration system, which consists of blood vessel clusters that are responsible for filtering the blood. Severe damage can lead to kidney failure or irreversible end-stage kidney disease, the condition which Nelson currently has.

Following a kidney transplant, the patient must be closely

monitored by a physician, as patients are at an increased risk of infection for 3-12 months after the surgery. Possible complications following a transplant can include blood flow issues, infection, rejection of the transplanted organ, and medication toxicity.

Nelson's wife has successfully petitioned immigration officials to allow her husband to be considered for permanent resident status so that he can receive his green card. However, because of his 30-year-old deportation order, he must leave the country during that process. Whether or not Nelson will be able to stay for the duration of his kidney transplantation and required recovery time is still unknown.

CHAPTER 6

ISABELLA

Isabella is a thirty-eight-year-old woman born in the Guatemalan town of Río Blanco, which translates to "White River." Río Blanco is characterized by its mountainous terrain in the San Marcos department of Guatemala. Isabella describes Río Blanco as a pretty place with people that were very simple and very poor. She came to the United States on February 14, 2007, in order to find work to pay for her children's studies back home in Guatemala, and she currently works as a cleaning lady to support herself and her family back home.

Isabella has a cataract in her eye and is using eye drops. She was also prescribed glasses that she needs for sun protection. Her doctor told her that if she doesn't use the glasses, she will eventually require an operation that costs anywhere from $3,000 to $5,000. A cataract occurs when the normally clear lens of the eye becomes cloudy. Eyeglasses and stronger lighting can help individuals deal with the effects of cataracts, but as the cloudiness becomes more problematic and interferes with daily activities, an individual may require cataract surgery. The symptoms of cataracts—including blurred or dim vision, difficulty with vision at night, sensitivity to light, need for brighter light while reading, fading or yellowing of colors, and double vision in a single eye—become more noticeable as the cataract grows larger. Cataracts form in the lens of the eye, which is positioned behind the iris. As an individual ages, the lenses become less flexible. In addition to a loss in flexibility, tissue breakdown within the lens also leads to clouding, which causes vision to become blurred due to the fact that it blocks light passing through the lens, therefore affecting the image that is able to reach the retina.[14]

She received her treatment at Open Door Port Chester. Open Door consists of various Family Medical Centers under one general foundation. The organization got its start in 1972 in the basement of the First Baptist Church in Port Chester, NY, and today it strives to provide high-quality medical care to individuals in Westchester and Putnam counties regardless of their ability to pay. Their values include access, affordability, community, efficiency, empowerment, and patient care. These values rest upon the tenets that quality health care is a right; that individuals deserve care regardless of their ability to pay; that access to health care benefits everyone in the community; that health care should be delivered timely and cost-effectively; that people can make good decisions when they are armed with the right information; and that people should come first.[15]

By ensuring that individuals are able to seek out medical care when necessary and therefore keep themselves in good health, children experience fewer absences from school, adults have fewer work absences, and there are fewer overall visits to local emergency rooms, thus lowering healthcare costs for the population as a whole. The empowerment piece of Open Door's mission is also extremely important. Given that Isabella is a native Spanish speaker, being able to receive medical advice and guidance in a way that is easy to comprehend is extremely important. Although her physician did not speak Spanish, there was a translator in the office to help Isabella understand the recommendations of the doctor.

Isabella was lucky enough to have her brother accompany her to her doctors' appointments. She said that if she has been alone, it would have been much more difficult to receive medical attention that she was comfortable with. Isabella appreciated the nurse who helped her, and she commented that her life would be different back in Guatemala because "they wouldn't have been able to help like they did in the United States."

Guatemala is the biggest country in Central America, and it also has one of the highest poverty levels in the world. The number of physicians is quite low, with 0.93 physicians per 1,000 people. According to the World Health Organization, countries with less than 23 healthcare professionals per 10,000 people are likely not to achieve acceptable coverage rates for primary care. Access to healthcare in Guatemala is extremely dependent on an individual's socioeconomic status and whether they live in an urban or rural environment.[16]

The town of Rio Blanco, where Isabella comes from, is a rural area. Despite efforts by the Guatemalan government to improve access to care, individuals in rural areas continue to have difficulty in accessing basic medical care. The World Bank estimates that basic health and nutrition services only meet fifty-four percent of the needs of the rural Guatemalan population.[17]

CHAPTER 7

SOFIA

Sofia is a three-year-old girl who was diagnosed with asthma. She recently went to the hospital for a lung infection (pneumonia), but she had experienced no serious problems in her first year of life. When she was one year old, she started wheezing. Following that, her parents brought her to the hospital because she was unable to breathe. Since then, she has been to the hospital on fifteen different occasions.

Asthma is a condition in which the airways become narrower and inflamed, and also produce a greater amount of mucus. This makes breathing more difficult and often triggers various symptoms such as wheezing, shortness of breath, and coughing.[18] Many individuals with asthma are barely bothered by their symptoms, but others are more severely affected and must follow treatment protocol in order to prevent an asthma attack. Asthma symptoms can be controlled; however, the overall condition cannot be cured and is something that individuals must learn to live with.

In addition to Sofia, her parents have four other children aged 3, 8, 12, and 14. Sofia is regularly exposed to marijuana smoke in her home, which together with other air pollutants may serve as a trigger for Sofia's asthma. Other irritants that may trigger allergies can also exacerbate asthma reactions. These include various airborne substances such as dust mites, pollen, pet dander, or mold spores; physical activity; respiratory infections; cold air; certain medications; sulfites and other preservatives that are added to food; and gastroesophageal reflux disease.

Sofia was at higher risk for having asthma because her mother also has it. Having a blood relative with asthma increases your own risk, as does being overweight, being a smoker, and having a separate allergic condition. Exposure to secondhand smoke, exhaust fumes, and chemicals present in various occupational settings can also increase the risk of asthma.

Sofia was receiving care at Cedarwood Clinic, an outpatient clinic associated with Westchester Medical Center. Individuals are treated there regardless of their insurance status and regardless of whether or not they are able to pay for the services. The medical students, residents, and fellows associated with the medical center are able to take a considerable lead in the treatment of the patients while being overseen by an attending physician. The majority of patients receiving care at this outpatient clinic have low socioeconomic status and are extremely grateful for the chance to get medical advice.

During a prior visit with the physician, Sofia's parents had been instructed to give her controller medications daily in order to prevent any flare-ups and avoid hospitalization. Sofia's parents did not speak any English and were living in a home together with various other relatives. On this occasion in the doctor's office, a remote translating service on an iPad was used to convey the information from the doctor to the parents. It became evident, based on the parents' descriptions of what medication Sofie was receiving on a regular basis, that her parents had not been following the physician's treatment plan that had been disclosed at an earlier appointment as instructed, likely because they did not understand the doctor's instructions due to health literacy issues.

Long-term control medications are extremely important in order to treat asthma and to ensure that the individual is able to maintain control over their condition and prevent a major swelling of the airway that would result in an asthma attack and subsequent hospitalization. Well-known long-term controller medications include Singulair, Advair, Symbicort, Pulmicort, Flovent, and QVAR.[19]

Her parent's lack of knowledge in relation to her illness and health condition led to many likely avoidable hospital visits. They were unable to understand the importance of delivering the controller medicine to Sofia on a daily basis, so when she experienced severe difficulty breathing, their first reaction was to bring her to the hospital. Health literacy is defined as the degree to which individuals are able to obtain, process, and understand basic health information and services that are needed to make appropriate health decisions. Health literacy affects an individual's ability to navigate the healthcare system, share personal information with their providers, and understand the risk associated with possible treatment options.[20]

Caring for patients who may not be able to follow the instructed medical advice they are given upon leaving the doctor's office is difficult because these individuals are put at risk for more severe illnesses that could have been avoided. Many immigrant families are unable to deliver the care recommended for their children as a result of not being able to understand or having more pressing issues, or full-time jobs that prevent them from being home to care for their children when necessary. Until Sofia is old enough to take her individual health matters into her own hands, her well-being remains at the mercy of her parents.

CHAPTER 8

COMMENTS FROM HEALTH CARE PROFESSIONALS

Lisa Albanese, R.N., the woman who employed Ana, said, "You are so right about patients needing advocates…. I remember asking her nurse what happens to patients without families. She shook her head and said, 'sometimes they just get lost,' meaning in the system and how their care is managed. I found that incredulous. Patients need advocates, whether it is family, a nurse, a social worker, or their doctor. It's so important!"

Even individuals responsible for providing care to a patient recognize the importance of having an advocate. Although it is a physician's duty to act in each patient's best interest, there are various potential obstacles that may prevent them from doing so. A physician may not recognize how emotional certain information may be for a patient to receive, and as a result, the patient may have trouble paying attention or focusing on a doctor's recommendations following the delivery of sensitive information.

For immigrant patients who seek medical attention, there are significant barriers that may affect their care, including limited English proficiency, unfamiliarity with the American healthcare system, and lack of health insurance. Medical providers that frequently care for undocumented immigrants may feel unequipped to address the many issues that affect this population. Doctors can be advocates for their immigrant patients in various ways: they may try to create welcoming environments in their clinics and hospitals, or they may emphasize confidentiality and offer reassurance that medical information will not be shared with immigration authorities. They can let patients know that it is safe to speak about sensitive topics, and they can make sure not to directly ask about immigration status or to document patient's immigration status within their medical records in order to reduce the stigma and avoid any possibility that ICE could discover their undocumented status.[21]

Physicians at Montefiore Hospital in the Bronx, NY have partnered with advocacy organizations to conduct forensic evaluations of refugees seeking asylum and individuals who are being detained in immigration detention centers. Such work can help identify patients who may be able to obtain legal immigration status.

Dr. Grivoyannis, a pediatric anesthesiologist at Johns Hopkins and volunteer with *Medicine Sans Frontieres* (Doctors without Borders), treated a 19-year-old boy in Jordan who came across the border and was unconscious after suffering a high-velocity trauma to the front of his head. He subsequently developed a severe infection in his brain, forcing the physicians working on his case to determine the best allocation of resources to this ICU patient. Dr. Grivoyannis was distraught over the fact that she was working on patients who had survived trauma, made it across the border under extremely dangerous conditions, recovered from severe infection, but now may never be able to walk again. It was very interesting to listen to an American physician who was able to experience providing care in foreign nations, and she was able to comment on the lack of resources compared to the US and how this "rationing of care" due to lack of supplies makes it harder to guarantee good health outcomes for a greater number of people.

When comparing the ability to provide care in an underdeveloped foreign nation versus the United States, it becomes clear that there are a greater number of resources and a larger number of individuals with medical knowledge in the US. When immigrants come to the United States, they are often able to benefit from this widespread knowledge, but the many barriers that they must overcome to provide care in the first place make it seem as if the lack of resources in the United States is comparable to that in the Middle East.

Immigrants and refugees are undoubtedly a vulnerable population. There is a large potential for health problems among these groups, as many of them have left countries with limited health care resources and where communicable diseases are regularly contracted by individuals. These groups are made even more vulnerable because they are not granted public health insurance upon entering the United States and cannot afford to pay for health care expenses out of pocket. A study that looked at the problem of medically uninsured immigrants in the United Kingdom, France, and Canada found it difficult to precisely quantify the effects upon immigrants and refugees without health insurance, but they did comment that there is evidence for this population experiencing poor health outcomes.[22]

Physicians responsible for treating Syrian refugees have documented their struggles, and it appears that social determinants of health have set this population at a major disadvantage. Refugees often have complex medical problems, and in host countries they face poor housing and sanitary environments, poor labor conditions, poor nutrition, and an inability to access medical care. In Syria, diseases like polio, which had been previously eradicated, have begun to reoccur. In addition, there is the fear that drug-resistant strains of tuberculosis may propagate in the region, as instances of tuberculosis have increased within Syria and neighboring countries.[23]

CHAPTER 9

LOOKING TO THE FUTURE

There are clear gaps in the system that need to be mended. Dr. Francis Ennis, an Orthopedic Surgeon in Connecticut, made the following comment: "The biggest issue that these immigrants face is that they don't have any reasonable health insurance. Therefore, they get all of their care in either an emergency room or urgent care type clinic. The cost of care in these centers is outrageous both in terms of what the patient has to pay, and when the patient doesn't pay, the cost to society. We really don't have a system in place to provide these underinsured or non-insured people reasonable medical care."

Dr. Lilia Cervantes, the physician who treated Hilda for her End Stage Renal Disease, commented on her relationship with Hilda, saying that they had become "close friends." After Hilda's passing, Dr. Cervantes decided that she needed to do something to change access to care in Colorado. She explained that doctors experience emotional burnout in different ways, and one of the reasons for burnout was the physician's inability to provide care to individuals in need of help due to current legislation. Dr. Cervantes encourages these individuals to turn to advocacy in order to reduce this moral distress.

Dr. Cervantes got involved in advocacy work to improve access to care. By completing the research necessary to illustrate this issue in the health care system, Dr. Cervantes hopes to save even more lives than she would be able to in her clinical work. She has spoken out on this issue and quickly realized that to be more effective in changing care for this community, she needed to provide evidence that change was necessary. She stopped doing advocacy work and decided to use her education in medicine to pursue research to change access to care throughout the US. Her research has been funded by the Robert Wood Johnson Foundation, the nation's largest public health philanthropy, which strives to "build a national Culture of Health that will enable all to live longer, healthier lives." While Dr. Cervantes still sees patients on occasion, her true passion now lies in health equity research and finding ways to improve access to care across the country. Health equity research focuses on solving community and population-based health and healthcare disparities. This research relies upon the recognition that health inequalities and disparities are rooted in the conditions in which people are born, grow, live, work, and age. The goal is to achieve a system where all people have the same opportunity to attain their full health potential.[24]

In order to expand coverage to undocumented immigrants, Dr. Cervantes believes we must modify policies that limit access to care. There are lots of social determinants of health that are not health-care related. These policy changes can begin with allowing immigrants who do not qualify for Medicaid due to their immigration status to receive care in a wider range of conditions under Emergency Medicaid. Unfortunately, even when insured, noncitizen immigrants and their children have poorer access to both ambulatory and emergency care compared to native citizens. Despite immigrants making up a large and growing portion of the American population, these individuals are disproportionately impoverished and uninsured.[25]

Additional research is needed on End Stage Renal Disease, and Dr. Cervantes is currently conducting studies on the cost-effectiveness of modifying policies as well as documenting the suffering that is experienced among caregivers. Besides End Stage Renal Disease, there are different research questions that can be asked for myriad other conditions, including liver disease, heart disease, and cancer.

When immigrant patients do receive care, physicians have identified self-advocacy as a major barrier. In Dr. Cervantes's experience, these patients tend to be very humble and do not advocate on their own behalf. They will not complain about things, ask for certain treatments, or pose questions. Besides a lack of self-advocacy, this patient group faces other barriers including social and cultural differences between the US and their native country. There is also a potential for patient stereotyping as certain clinicians may assume an immigrant patient wants a certain type of care. Patients also may face educational, health literacy, language, and socioeconomic barriers. These barriers all point to the idea of "social determinants of health."

I had the chance to speak with Family Health Care Network (FHCN), a nonprofit community-based organization that operates 31 sites in California. This organization has grown from a small outpatient health center serving a farmworker community to a multi-site primary care network serving 253,850 patients. They are currently one of the largest providers of care to underserved populations in the country, and they represent a viable model of community health care that reduces health disparities and improves health status among communities in need. Family Health Care Network has worked to advance the development of community-based primary health care delivery systems to address the health care needs of underserved and vulnerable populations. They operate on the belief that everyone has the right to the highest quality health care and to be treated with dignity and respect regardless of their ability to pay.

Their mission to provide quality health care to everyone in the communities they serve regardless of financial constraints allows immigrants greater access to care as well as higher-quality care compared to what they would be able to receive in different locations throughout the US. Family Health Care Network has also been able to break down language barriers and other barriers to access. In terms of short-term impact, FHCN helps their patients avoid episodic emergency room treatment, thus alleviating the family pressure that was caused by Hilda's inability to receive dialysis when not in a state of emergency. In terms of their long-term impact, FHCN strives to provide a home base for medical care that is centered and coordinated for their patients.[26]

Another organization with a strong resemblance to FHCN, but with a greater focus on the integration of immigrants into the community, is Neighbors Link in New York's Westchester County. Many immigrants struggle when faced with the task of integrating into a new community, and Neighbors Link strives to meet this need. Neighbors Link, an office for New Americans Opportunity Center, has helped 344 people apply for citizenship since April 2016.[27] They provide trainings to local police forces that address issues of cultural differences, cultural awareness, and institutional bias with the goal of improving communication and fostering trust between social groups. In 2018, they served 4,000 immigrants, with over 800 individuals participating in English as a Second Language (ESL) classes. They facilitated jobs for nearly 600 workers, handled 172 complex legal cases, and helped 125 people receive legal assistance when applying for US citizenship or DACA status.

The Association of American Medical Colleges publishes the core competencies for entering medical students online, and one of these is "cultural competence." It is vital that physicians are properly able to address the concerns of and treat patients from a cultural background different from their own. This sensitive care is necessary for the integration of these patients into the US health care system. It is important that a physician does not stereotype or generalize when dealing with a patient of a certain ethnic background.

CHAPTER 10

THE IMPORTANCE OF ADVOCACY DURING CARE

An article in the journal *Nursing Critical Care* details a nurse's personal experience serving as an advocate for a geriatric patient. Her advocacy took the form of making sure her 98-year-old patient, a resident at a costly facility, did not keep receiving eggs on her breakfast tray even though she was allergic to them. "This experience taught me a valuable lesson in patient advocacy. By taking a stand and changing something as simple as her breakfast, I helped Mrs. K feel more in control of her life. Patient advocacy also can avert potentially serious complications, such as a food allergy or an adverse medication reaction... I learned two powerful lessons: addressing concerns gets results, and you always need to be a voice for your patients, whether it's for their physical health or their breakfast."[28]

The National Cancer Institute at the National Institutes of Health defines a patient advocate as an individual who plays a role in guiding a patient through the healthcare system. This job includes assisting the patient through the screening, diagnosis, treatment, and follow-up stages of a medical condition. A patient advocate ensures that the patient is able to successfully communicate with their health care provider in order to get all the information necessary to make informed decisions about the care that they are to receive.[29]

Everyone needs an advocate. According to Nancy Brook, nurse practitioner, UCSF faculty member, and patient advocate through Stanford Healthcare, "Our health care system isn't perfect and having a patient advocate is important to get the proper care. By educating yourself and taking action, you can go from hopeless to hopeful." Brook suggested that individuals who are unable to act as their own advocate find one, perhaps a family member, friend, volunteer, social worker, or patient advocate provided by the hospital. Brook recommends preparing for all doctor and test appointments by writing down questions for the physician ahead of time; this will ensure that any concerns are addressed during face-to-face meetings with the doctor. Another piece of advice offered by Brook was to not feel rushed into decisions. Even if a physician says you need to start treatment for a certain condition immediately, do your research or have a family member help you determine what the best treatment is for you. Finally, taking notes while speaking with the doctor, even if you are acting as your own advocate, can help you ensure that you aren't missing any important information that was relayed during your appointment.[30]

The elderly perhaps have the most potential benefit to gain from a patient advocate. When a doctor delivers a serious diagnosis to a patient, it is hard for them to listen carefully and be able to ask important questions. Strong emotions such as fear and shock often make it extremely difficult to listen to exactly what the physician is saying and make it even harder to digest and comprehend the information that is being presented. It is during this time that having a patient advocate—an extra set of eyes, mouth, and ears—can prove incredibly beneficial. The American Association of Retired Persons documented research that shows that in order to receive high-quality health care an individual must take an active role in the decisions about their care.[31] At times when an individual may be distracted or unable to fully comprehend, it is necessary to have a supportive figure that will aid the patient in making an informed choice.

CHAPTER 11

SOCIAL DETERMINANTS OF HEALTH

I recently went to a talk on my college campus given by Robert Hummer, professor of sociology at the University of North Carolina at Chapel Hill. His talk was the keynote address of a two-day conference called "Deep Wounds: Social Determinants of Health Inequality." His address focused on the wide-ranging causes of a downturn in American life expectancy, arguing that the causes are "deeper, broader, more demographically diverse, more epidemiologically complex and more institutionalized than what the media portrays and what most policymakers are working on."

When it comes to immigrants arriving in America, the social determinants of health are incredibly important in assessing the health outcomes that they experience. Typically, when first arriving to America, these individuals may not have a job, have low income, etc. Their neighborhood and physical environment will likely not be the safest or cleanest. In addition, their level of education, literacy in English, and ability to communicate will make it more difficult for them to properly express themselves in the healthcare setting. All of these social factors have a direct determination on their healthcare outcomes.

I attended another talk given by Dr. T Colin Campbell, a Cornell

University professor, called "Nutrition as Medicine." He stated that health is best achieved by eating the right foods and that the leading cause of death is nutritional ignorance. When individuals do not have access to healthy food options and are forced to eat the cheapest thing availability, their health is at risk. This may certainly be the case among many recent immigrants who may not have access to a steady supply of nutritious, healthy food options.

When I spoke with Dr. Cervantes, the physician at the UC Boulder affiliated hospital who has provided care to undocumented immigrants, and asked her what the largest barrier to care that these immigrants faced was, she responded with the social determinants of health. These individuals are at a disadvantage due to their socioeconomic status and their lack of citizenship. Dr. Cervantes also brought up the idea of cultural barriers, which serve as a potential point of clinician unfairness based on preexisting stereotypes. She said, "Our health is also determined in part by access to social and economic opportunities; the resources and supports available in our homes, neighborhoods, and communities; the quality of our schooling; the safety of our workplaces; the cleanliness of our water, food, and air; and the nature of our social interactions and relationships. The conditions in which we live explain in part why some Americans are healthier than others and why Americans more generally are not as healthy as they could be."

CHAPTER 12

US HEALTH CARE RESTRICTIONS

Legal immigrants must wait five years after entering the United States in order to receive Medicaid. In addition, uninsured people receive about fifty percent less medical care than insured people. This means that many immigrants are not getting care when they need it. It is possible that they have no usual source of care, they have postponed seeking care due to cost, they have gone without needed care due to cost, and/or they have postponed or did not get a needed prescription drug due to cost.[32] The 2017 Current Population Survey found that Hispanics are the demographic most likely to be uninsured when looking at insurance coverage by race and ethnicity. The United States is one of the few high-income countries that does not provide universal health insurance. In 2019, the individual mandate under the Affordable Care Act required all individuals to buy health insurance or face a fine (the fine will be eliminated in 2019). Requiring individuals to buy health insurance actually has a positive long-term effect, as it makes the pool of individuals buying into the healthcare market larger and thus causes lower medical spending as a result of more individuals contributing to the cost of the medical care received by individuals who need it more frequently.

It is predicted that immigrants comprise about thirty percent of uninsured individuals in the United States.[33] Before 2019, the Patient Protection and Affordable Care Act (ACA) stated that documented immigrants that had lived in the United States for less than five years were subject to the individual mandate but were ineligible for Medicaid, causing them to either buy health insurance on the exchanges or pay the fine for not purchasing insurance.[34]

Among the reasons for low health care utilization among immigrants, besides socioeconomic and demographic factors, is something known as "immigrant self-selection."[35] In order to leave their country of origin, it is necessary that immigrants be in decent physical health at the time of their relocation, thus causing them to have higher overall health than the average health experienced in the country they are coming from. This lowers the perceived need for health care upon arriving in the US.

CHAPTER 13

RATIONALIZING THE NEED FOR ACCESS TO CARE

Many individuals may see providing immigrants with better care as a drain on the economy, especially because the government is not getting any return in taxes in order to offset the revenue. This is a common misconception, as undocumented immigrants are indeed paying taxes even though they may not be official US citizens.

In countries with anti-immigration policies (and therefore a lack of beneficial healthcare strategies), there is a clear effect on access to health services. Additionally, immigrants are impacted by mental health outcomes, such as depression, anxiety, and post-traumatic stress disorder. Despite few longitudinal studies to date, a possible connection between a lack of healthcare options for migrants and physical health outcomes such as autism, hypertension, cardiovascular disease, low birth weight, and prematurity are theorized to exist.[36]

When undocumented migrants are granted refugee status, they are allowed greater access to health services. However, when they do not receive such treatment as a result of policy decisions, they suffer due to laws that restrict their right to access health services and those that grant minimum rights to health services.

The current global financial crisis has led to strict immigration policies and laws that have affected immigrants' access to HIV and

STI screenings and care, including prenatal care services. In addition, they have been restricted from accessing basic health care services, such as emergency care. The exclusion of these immigrants from vital services due to their "undocumented" status is disheartening and dangerous. In the United States, various state governments have enforced policies that allow undocumented immigrants to only receive immigrant care when their condition is "immediate or urgent." Such emergency care is dangerous for the health of the patient and puts a greater strain on hospital resources than receiving periodic care.

In the few countries that entitle undocumented immigrants' access to care beyond emergency care, specifically primary and secondary care, better overall health is extremely visible.

According to Dr. Chrisia Noulas, who works in General Pediatrics at Maria Ferari Children's Hospital in Valhalla, NY, part of the resident curriculum is to read the book *Enrique's Journey* by Sonia Nazario, which tells the tale of a 17-year-old boy who travels from Honduras to the United States in search of his mother. Gaining a general understanding of the damaging events these individuals have gone through is the first step to being able to provide useful and appropriate medical care, most of which has to do with past abuse and the stress that comes along with surviving traumatic experiences.

Dr. Noulas had the opportunity to attend a children's advocacy conference (NYSPAC) which was largely focused on immigrant health: "During discussions, physicians stated that there is a lot of reluctance [from immigrants] to seek medical health because of fear and distrust of 'the systems.' Hospitals had been regarded as safe havens in the past; however, two doctors noted that ICE had made a physical presence at the entrance of Mt. Sinai Hospital in New York and they also tried to open a satellite office outside of Northwell Health. Thankfully these were short-lived, but the message was sent." Northwell Health is a network of hospitals that has earned the title of New York's largest healthcare provider.

At this conference, the idea of "sanctuary doctoring" was presented, although it is difficult to promote in this political climate. This idea and necessary materials were developed in order to help physicians and health care professionals to meet the immediate needs of their patients who may be undocumented or who have close family that is undocumented.[37] Doctors at Northwell Health have adopted this technique and have begun wearing pins that say: "Immigration worries? Talk to me."

The presenter at the conference, Dr. Omolara Uwemedino, M.D., MPH, discussed her article in *Pediatrics* entitled "A Dream Deferred: Ending DACA Threatens Children, Families, and Communities." Within this article, the authors make a plea. "We encourage pediatricians to recognize the powerful impact of family immigration status as a social determinant of health. Identifying legal concerns during visits, including those regarding immigration, can help to start the conversation in a setting often considered a rare "safe space" and reinforces the value of medical-legal partnerships that assist families with immigration concerns. Identifying mental health problems and providing care with referrals can support youth coping strategies and improve their psychological well-being. Connecting families to resources addressing social needs can reduce stress and enhance health outcomes. Making pediatric practices welcoming to all patients, including children in immigrant families, can foster trust in the health care system."[38]

An advocacy group by the name of CCC (Citizen's Committee for Children) discussed some legislation including *Coverage for All* (A. 5974/S.3900) which includes coverage for immigrants, and another law that ensures that Temporary Protected Status Holders (TPS) are eligible for Medicaid even after their TPS is terminated (A.3316/S.1809). Following this, an attorney and professor from Columbia brought up some disheartening facts in regards to immigrants: (1) between October 2014 and July 2018, the Department of Health and Human Services received 4,556 complaints of sexual abuse, and the Department of Justice received

1309 complaints, and (2) globally, 40 million people are affected by trafficking, forced labor, and forced marriage, with 1 in 4 under the age of 18.

The obstacles faced by unaccompanied alien children (UAC) are rather disheartening. Physicians for human rights have filed complaints with various detention centers. In one instance, there was a "16-month-old baby who lost a third of his body weight over 10 days from an untreated diarrheal disease, yet was never given IV fluids." In another facility, "numerous children were vaccinated with adult doses of a vaccine as providers were not familiar with labels." The legislation for unaccompanied minors has continually been changing and there is hope that these children will receive the protection that they need, especially if we are able to inspire more people to advocate.

CHAPTER 14

COMPARISON WITH DENMARK

All over the world, countries are struggling to provide health care to uninsured individuals, even in countries that offer free health services to their citizens and legal residents. The health care system in Denmark is internationally renowned for its widespread coverage made possible by Denmark's welfare state. I had the chance to visit the Red Cross Health Clinic located in Copenhagen, Denmark, where I learned a great deal about the completely free care that is provided to undocumented migrants. I spoke with Viki, the director of the clinic, as well as Ulla, a retired General Practitioner who volunteers at the clinic twice a month.

The clinic is open Monday, Wednesday, and Thursday. On Monday there are two volunteer doctors on duty, on Wednesday there is a doctor and a midwife, and on Thursday there is a doctor and a dentist or a physical therapist. In Denmark, you need what is called a CPR number in order to get access to free health services. Many immigrants come to Denmark in order to try to find jobs to survive, but many can't find legal jobs, which in turn makes it hard for them to find an apartment to rent because it is expensive.

Individuals within the European Union are able to freely move between countries, but problems arise when the individual is unable to afford a place to live and then quickly becomes either homeless or a migrant.

The Red Cross Health Clinic in Copenhagen was established out of the belief that all people should have access to healthcare. Most people receiving care at the clinic are not legal citizens of Denmark. Red Cross is a private organization, so they are unable to get money from the state. It is the responsibility of the director of the clinic to raise funds, and they are also able to receive some money from the international Red Cross foundation. The Red Cross has about 220 partnerships, as well as second-hand shops within the city that use their sales to raise money for the clinic. The actual costs of running the clinic are rather inexpensive due to the heavy reliance on volunteers. It takes about 2.8 million Danish Kroner (about 426,000 USD) a year to run the clinic in Copenhagen and in Aarhus, the second-largest city in Denmark. Many of the volunteer doctors have a full-time job as well, so they are only required to come in and work once a month.

In terms of language barriers, there is a list of translators that the physicians are able to call if they are unable to communicate with their patients. The clinic runs into problems with communication despite the existence of this help, especially when their patient is of the Roma people, commonly known across Europe as Gypsies. Many of the Roma people that come to Denmark face exclusion and discrimination.

The largest group seeking care in the clinic are African immigrants. For many years the second largest group was EU citizens from Eastern Europe (who tended to be poor and uneducated and traveled between EU countries looking for work), but now the second largest group is from Asia. There are many au pairs from the Philippines that come to Denmark and choose to stay in order to work in cleaning and housekeeping to send money back to their families. In addition, there are many Asian men who work illegal jobs in Denmark. Despite the widespread patient backgrounds, Viki was happy to announce there are no conflicts in the clinic: "The [patients] are sitting together side by side from different countries and there are no problems."

The political parties in Denmark know about the work that the clinic is doing, but they don't want to be involved or incur any costs for the services the clinic provides. It appears that as long as the Red Cross is taking care of it themselves, they are free to continue with their work. The director of the clinic puts together annual reports containing statistics about where the patients come from, their ages, and their diseases, and so on. The first annual report was sent to the health minister and put on the website. In the following years, Viki decided she didn't want the report published in the news because she wants to avoid publicity. Given current anti-immigrant sentiment in Denmark, she fears that too much publicity may eventually result in a new law that would prohibit the existence of the clinic.

As a result, the clinic relies on word-of-mouth to reach the at-risk populations. Ulla explained, "The Red Cross doesn't have many outreach materials. They [those that work there] don't talk about it much." Thankfully, the Red Cross clinic works alongside various different organizations in Denmark, so when the clinic announced its opening in August 2011, many of the other social organizations that work with migrants were able to make referrals. Before the clinic opened, Viki invited these organizations to a meeting to exchange information and ideas. She made flyers in sixteen different languages with info about the opening hours and distributed them to the organizations so that she could pick up the flyers and give them to migrants as needed. Today, knowledge about the clinic is mostly passed from person to person. The migrants tell each other where they can go for shelter, for food, and, in this case, for health services. Migrants are able to find information about the clinic on the website, but the address is not posted in order to keep out people who don't require services, including the "journalists who are busy trying to find a good story." All of this is undertaken in order to ensure the protection of their patients.

The Red Cross Health Clinic has also formed a relationship with the police in order to ensure the safety of their patients. Building trust with the police lessens the likelihood that their patients will be arrested due to their lack of citizenship status. In one instance, before Christmas last year Viki heard that the police were standing outside the clinic. These were not local police, but from a special government department. Viki couldn't do anything about it, so she called the general secretary of the Red Cross and set up a meeting with the director of the police in Copenhagen to explain their purpose in the community.

Ulla said, "The police know [the clinic] is there but they don't do anything about it. The police can come and take the patients and put them in jail because they are illegal. Last year [the police] took 15 people when they walked out of the clinic and sent them home or to jail. I don't think it will happen again but after that less [sic] people came to the clinic because they were scared it would happen again, but now it is back to normal."

This fear is present even in the United States, where a recent study found that undocumented Mexican immigrants were twenty-seven percent less likely to have visited a doctor in the previous year compared to documented immigrants. They were also thirty-five percent less likely than documented immigrants to have a regular source of care.[39] The fact of the matter is that it's impossible to tell the police to stay away from the clinic. However, through explaining the job of the clinic and the importance of allowing the undocumented migrants to receive the proper treatment, the police become a little more understanding.

In response to my question about mental health problems such as anxiety and depression among immigrants, Viki informed me that once a month a psychiatrist comes to the clinic. There is also a psychologist, yet people don't ask for the psychologist much. She explained that the patient group is different in Copenhagen and in Aarhus, with the immigrants in Aarhus seeking out psychological help much more frequently. In Aarhus, the individuals have a home where they can live, and they have a family. She theorized that because these individuals have a platform and a home base, it is easier for them to examine other issues besides just physical ailments. In comparison, the patient population in Copenhagen is more likely to be homeless and seeking care for an immediate issue. The individuals living on the streets are bending over every day picking up plastic bottles to turn in for cash, or they are in the kitchen doing hard work all day that causes their muscles to hurt. Viki explained that she tells them to go to the physical therapist, but they think that all they need for their pain is a doctor to prescribe them pills.

Under Danish health law, all people have full access to health service in a time of emergency. If patients come into the hospital with an urgent issue, the physicians at the clinic are able to immediately refer them to the hospital. About two-to-four people per month are sent to the hospital. For example, a Polish immigrant came to the clinic with a large infection behind his knee. Because the clinic did not have the resources to take care of the infection on-site, the doctor called the hospital and he was sent there. Viki added, "[The immigrants] are treated very well [at the hospital]."

The director said the purpose of the clinic was "for health care, not prevention." The clinic provides vaccinations to children, but not for adults. All child vaccinations can be received free of charge in Denmark, and adults can buy the vaccine at the pharmacy on their own and bring it to the clinic to be administered. The fact that the clinic's purpose is not for prevention is interesting, considering that Denmark is big on preventative care; they have a large public health system and don't have the funds to provide emergency care to everyone. Providing lower-cost preventative care is much more cost-effective than forgoing those health services. Treating patients when they present with a serious condition requires greater medical spending that could have been avoided with preventative care.

In Denmark, individuals are able to receive free abortions up until week twelve of pregnancy. At the clinic, doctors are able to carry out medical abortions, with pills, up to eight weeks of pregnancy.

After this time period, patients must go to the hospital and pay for it themselves since it is not considered an emergency situation.

In terms of pregnancy care, women are unable to have scans conducted but can come in for normal examinations with a midwife. Since birth is considered an emergency situation, the individuals are able to deliver at the nearest hospital; however, after the fact the hospital is allowed to send a bill to the patient that they are obligated to pay. For this reason, the Red Cross does not send them to the hospital, or the hospital bill may be charged to the clinic.

"What we see here is just the tip of the iceberg," said Viki. "Even though this is just a fraction of it, it is showing that this is an urgent issue and we need to stay open."

It's impossible to know how the number of immigrants she is seeing in the clinic compares to those that she is not seeing. One article came out with an estimate that there were at least 30,000 immigrants in Denmark, and Danes were appalled that there were so many. In the following years, the number has gone down, perhaps only as a result of political pressure to undervalue the true number. It is difficult to arrive at a more accurate number of immigrants within Denmark because the migrants are "always moving around" and are therefore hard to count.

Despite not being able to pinpoint definite figures, the success of the clinic is obvious and there are hopes to open two more mini-clinics in Odense and Aalborg, two other Danish cities. Viki stated, "The two clinics right now are not enough because we know that migrants are all over." These issues are widespread, in both the city and the countryside, and it is clear that the work of the volunteers at the clinic is making an undeniably positive impact on the health of the immigrants it serves.

CHAPTER 15

CONCLUSION

During the process of writing this book, I have been amazed by the powerful stories that have been shared with me. From a Hungarian immigrant who had a heart attack and was treated in the hospital for four days without insurance to later receive a $90,000 bill that she will pay for the rest of her life, to a young boy from Guatemala with severe autism who had no access to medication for his behavioral issues and was ultimately denied brain surgery necessary to relieve his seizures because it was not considered a life-threatening condition, these stories demonstrate the precariousness of immigrant health outcomes in the US.

A movie recently played at the Jacob Burns Film Festival entitled "A Film for a Purpose," which documented an alliance of grandmothers who have gone to the US/Mexico border to create an "overground" railroad to help young children who are separated from their families and attend to their medical needs. The strong acts of hatred in our world are met with great acts of love and support, and this is just one of those examples.

There seems to be a common thread in the firsthand stories documented in the opening chapters of this book. All of the patients had some companion who was there for them during their healthcare journey, whether it was a family member, a friend, or a social worker.

Physicians and other health care professionals across the United States are extremely capable and well-educated individuals; however, in order to ensure the most well-rounded care, the patient must feel comfortable and have someone that they trust by their side who is able to aid them in the difficult process of digesting medical information and recommendations.

Upon my visit to the Medical University of Vienna Hospital, a neurosurgeon who had completed a fellowship at the Mayo Clinic in Minnesota said the following: "I was offered a position to stay in the United States and practice there, but I chose to come back to Austria because although my salary might not be as high, in Austria I am not faced with the decision of who I can and cannot treat. That is why someone becomes a doctor, so that they are able to treat everyone." These words resonated with me. A physician takes the Hippocratic Oath, swearing that they will "…apply, for the benefit of the sick, all measures [that] are required…." They also attest the following: "I will remember that I remain a member of society, with special obligations to *all* my fellow human beings…."

A physician should not have to pay attention to politics when deciding who they will provide care to. When faced with saving another human's life, one cannot be concerned with who the person is, where they come from, and how they ended up in this place in their time of need. A priest is treated the same as a criminal or terrorist, the same as a successful businessman, the same as the president of our country. A pediatric neurologist at Bethesda Children's Hospital in Budapest, Hungary, expressed similar concerns after sharing that his brother is an oncologist in Connecticut who is unable to take care of every patient who comes to his office: "I might not be able to provide the absolute best care to every patient due to a lack of resources, but at least I am able to treat every patient." Hungary has a National Health Insurance that is funded by taxes, and the doctor explained it as a "low-financed but widely covered system."

There are many doctors in the United States who struggle with the inability to provide care to individuals in need as a result of legislation, which Dr. Cervantes identified as a source of burnout. An emergency room doctor in Syracuse, New York explained that immigrants come to the ER for minor things, but he knows the real reason they come is to get out of the cold because they don't have shelter. He is faced with a moral dilemma: does he kick them out of the emergency room, putting them and their children back out on the streets, or does he allow them to stay in the emergency room? When you think of an answer, you must keep in mind that as an emergency room doctor your goal is to clear the beds as quickly as possible.

In Denmark, the Red Cross Health Clinic that I discussed was based on international human rights, especially the right for all people to receive health care. A handout from the clinic clearly states: "The Members of the Danish Medical Association want to fulfill the Hippocratic Oath which commits to provide medical care to all people. The idea to build a health clinic for undocumented migrants is inspired by research in Norway and Sweden, where they have had clinics for undocumented migrants associated with Red Cross." Many immigrants must hide from the police and are afraid to receive health care, so they forgo needed medical treatments and do not get vaccinated to prevent certain diseases. Many individuals are sick and are in danger of harming themselves or infecting those around them.

It is from this public health perspective that I first became intrigued about the experiences of immigrants within the US health care system. When I saw the young girl receiving tuberculosis treatment free of charge from the US Department of Health, I thought we as a country were just being kind because she was all alone. I didn't even think about the risk of her infecting US citizens who would then need to go seek out medical treatment. Whether you agree that immigrants who are uninsured should be provided care or not, one thing that can be agreed upon is that when more members of society are healthy, it benefits everyone.

Another interesting consideration is that few doctors are

immigrants themselves, which constrains both doctors and patients. The physicians are members of different classes, they live in different areas, they have different social networks, and even when patient and doctor do meet there are various factors that prevent the doctors from providing care that aligns with the needs of the patient. Perhaps, by having a culturally diverse health center, the care that is administered will be more likely to be appropriate and sensitive to immigrant patients.[40] Another mode of action may be the formation of partnerships between health centers and immigrant groups in order to foster a sense of trust and serve as a source of information for patients whose unfamiliarity with the health care system results in a barrier to access.

Even when patients do have health care coverage, this does not immediately translate into access to the medical care that they are entitled to. When patients are unfamiliar with the system, including factors such as price, method of payment, patient-physician relation, they are much less likely to receive care than their more familiar counterparts. In Denmark, for example, the system functions much differently. The general practitioner functions as a gatekeeper and their referral is needed in order to be able to make an appointment with a specialist. Because there is a national health system where the majority of health services are free of cost, you must call a number for an immediate concern. You are unable to schedule a same-day sick appointment at your doctor's office due to long queues and you cannot show up at the hospital unless you are in a definite state of emergency.

During my travels through Europe, I have found myself in fear of the unknown and an overwhelming feeling that I do not belong in each country where my ears fill with sounds, syllables, and intonations that I am unable to produce with my own tongue. Even so, I am always able to find some English signs or writing, or someone who can communicate with me in my own native language. I can't help but think about if my grandparents and relatives with a different mother tongue experienced that same sense of dis-belonging. No matter where you come from, arriving in a new place is difficult. Now imagine having some physical ailment that you then must receive treatment for on top of your already precarious position.

Immigrants are immediately at a higher risk for psychological problems as a result of the problems that they experience when integrating into an unfamiliar community. In the health care setting, they must rely on translators, which results in a very unnatural interaction between doctor and patient. The medical jargon is complicated to understand and often requires later research by the patient or another individual accompanying them during their care.

In painting this picture, the main purpose is to force us to consider the struggles these individuals face—struggles that never cross the minds of native citizens who are comfortable in the health care setting. The point of this book is to highlight the great organizations that have been created to provide high-quality medical care to individuals who would be unable to receive it otherwise. It pays tribute to all the advocates—the family members, companions, friends, confidants—who support patients through their difficult times. It recognizes the physicians and other health care professionals that have been faced with difficult decisions but have used their medical training and their knowledge to do good and to inspire change for the future of medical care. It showcases the brave individuals who were forced to embark on a journey that they never asked to be a part of, yet who remained resilient despite the obstacles that emerged before them. It calls upon future leaders who will advocate for better medical care for immigrants and for changes that will make the system more comprehensive, accessible, and transparent than it is today.

In the speech that I gave at my 2016 high school graduation ceremony, I challenged my classmates to be aware of their surroundings and to attempt to understand the struggle of others. To open the cover of each metaphorical book and see what is inside, the pages that make up a story rich with raw experience. To go beyond the surface and actually document the struggles that have been felt by individuals in our same towns, same states, or same country. I asked my classmates: "Why don't we force ourselves to learn what people halfway around the world are suffering through?" Just a few years ago, I was too naïve to realize that there are people suffering right next to us, maybe even among us in our graduating class. I thought these issues of inequality, unacceptance, and marginalization only plagued places far from where I myself called home.

There is so much that we can do in our own communities to influence the quality of care that immigrants are able to receive. I told my class that "there is no way that we can determine our role in society if we are unable to open our eyes and really think about what is lacking." We need a general basis of knowledge to serve us as a foundation for making even the smallest amount of meaningful change. Today, however, I feel as though there is no excuse for not taking a stance. The dialogue around immigration is lengthy and dense, and as members of society it is our duty to decide what type of future we want for the following generations and what type of action we will take to achieve that future.

ACKNOWLEDGEMENTS

There is a never-ending list of people to thank for this book, but most important is the positive influence that they have had on my life, which has resulted in me even having this opportunity.

First, my family. Mom and Dad, thank you for everything. I owe all my success to the opportunities you have provided me. Thank you for giving me the chance to discover myself and my passions both at Cornell, in Copenhagen, and in all my future endeavors. To Arianna and Melina for being the best friends I could ever ask for. Thank you to my Yiayia Helen and Papou John who are the most supportive grandparents and have always so generously ensured that I experienced all that this world has to offer, something which has helped shaped me on my journey to adulthood. And to my "Big Fat Greek" extended family for being loud and full of love, especially my Uncle Alex who was suddenly taken from us but whose laugh and smile I will never forget.

To my friends who provide me with a source of laughter and a constant stream of happiness.

To the doctors that I have shadowed and interacted with who have solidified my passion for medicine and showed me through their work the happiness that can result from helping others.

To my teachers at Blind Brook High School and professors at Cornell that have challenged me and fostered my love of learning.

Thank you.

ENDNOTES

1   Center for Children and Families. "Immigrants & Affordable Health Insurance in Colorado." October 14, 2016. https://www.coloradohealth. org/sites/default/files/documents/2017-01/Immigrant Eligibility.pdf.

2   Ku, Leighton, and Sheetal Matani. "Left Out: Immigrants' Access To Health Care And Insurance." Health Affairs. Accessed February 5, 2019. https://www.healthaffairs.org/doi/full/10.1377/hlthaff.20.1.247.

3   Bustamante, Arturo Vargas, Philip J. Van der Wees. "Integrating Immigrants into the US Health System." *American Medical Association Journal of Ethics* 14, no. 4 (April 2012):318-323.

4   American Cancer Society. "Ovarian Cancer Treatment | How to Treat Ovarian Cancer." Accessed December 12, 2018. https://www.cancer.org/cancer/ovarian-cancer/treating.html.

5   Bouloutza, Penny. "A Greek Malady: Too Many Doctors, Too Few GPs." Kathimerini English Edition. September 05, 2017. http://www.ekathimerini.com/221371/article/ekathimerini/community/a-greek-malady-too-many-doctors-too-few-gps.

6   HealthManagement.org. "An Overview of the Healthcare System in Greece." HealthManagement. April 03, 2019. https://healthmanagement.org/c/imaging/issuearticle/an-overview-of-the-healthcare-system-in-greece-1.

7   Kalampokas, Emmanouil, Theodoros Kalampokas, and Christos Damaskos. "Primary Vaginal Melanoma, A Rare and Aggressive Entity. A Case Report and Review of the Literature." *In Vivo* 21, no.1 (January 2017): 133-139. https://doi.org/10.21873/invivo.11036.

8   Wolters Kluwer Health. "Treatment Approach and Outcomes of Vaginal Melanoma." Accessed November 14, 2018. https://journals.lww.com/ijgc/fulltext/2013/10000/Treatment_Approach_and_Outcomes_of_Vaginal.23.aspx.

9   American Cancer Society. "What Is Cancer Immunotherapy?" Accessed February 7, 2019. https://www.cancer.org/treatment/treatments-and-side-effects/treatment-types/immunotherapy/what-is-immunotherapy.html.

10   Migrationpolicy.org. "State Demographics Data - CO." November 01, 2018. http://www.migrationpolicy.org/data/state-profiles/state/demographics/CO.

11   Center for Children and Families. "Immigrants & Affordable Health Insurance in Colorado." October 14, 2016. https://www.coloradohealth.org/sites/default/files/documents/2017-01/Immigrant Eligibility.pdf.

12   Paniagua, Ramón, Alfonso Ramos, Rosaura Fabian, Jesús Lagunas, and Dante Amato. "Chronic Kidney Disease and Dialysis in Mexico." *Peritoneal Dialysis International: Journal of the International Society for Peritoneal Dialysis* 27, no.4 (July 2007): 405-9.

13   NBC News. "How Providing Unequal Care to Immigrant Patients Contributes to Doctor Burnout." June 1, 2018. https://www.nbcnews.com/health/health-care/another-cause-doctor-burnout-being-forced-give-immigrants-unequal-care-n878856.

14   Mayo Clinic. "Cataracts." June 23, 2018. https://www.mayoclinic.org/diseases-conditions/cataracts/symptoms-causes/syc-20353790.

15   Open Door Family Medical Centers. "Mission, Vision, Values." Accessed January 15, 2019. https://www.opendoormedical.org/about-us/mission-vision-values/.

16   Centers for Disease Control and Prevention. "Central American Refugee Health Profiles." Accessed January 21, 2019. https://www.cdc.gov/immigrantrefugeehealth/profiles/central-american/healthcare-diet/index.html.

17   World Bank. "Universal Healthcare on the rise in Latin America". February 14, 2013. https://www.worldbank.org/en/news/feature/2013/02/14/universal-healthcare-latin-america

18   Mayo Clinic. "Asthma." September 13, 2018. https://www.mayoclinic.org/diseases-conditions/asthma/symptoms-causes/syc-20369653.

19   Asthma Initiative of Michigan (AIM). "Long-Term Control Medications Used to Treat Asthma." Accessed March 3, 2019. https://getasthmahelp.org/ltc-medications.aspx.

20   U.S. Department of Health and Human Services, Office of Disease Prevention and Health Promotion. "Quick Guide to Health Literacy." Accessed November 13, 2019. https://health.gov/communication/literacy/quickguide/factsbasic.htm.

21 Ross, Jonathan. "How Doctors Can Be Immigration Activists." The Doctor's Tablet. March 22, 2018. http://blogs.einstein.yu.edu/how-doctors-can-be-immigration-activists/.

22 Caulford, Paul, and Yasmin Vali. "Providing Health Care to Medically Uninsured Immigrants and Refugees." *Canadian Medical Association Journal* 174, no.9 (April 2006): 1253-4. https://doi.org/10.1503/cmaj.051206.

23 Karasapan, Omer, and Omer Karasapan. "The Challenges in Providing Health Care to Syrian Refugees." Brookings. November 15, 2018. https://www.brookings.edu/blog/future-development/2018/11/15/the-challenges-in-providing-health-care-to-syrian-refugees/.

24 "About Health Equity Research and Policy." Association of American Medical Colleges. Accessed January 4, 2019. https://www.aamc.org/initiatives/research/healthequity/348640/abouthealthequity.html.

25 Ku, Leighton, and Sheetal Matani. "Left Out: Immigrants' Access To Health Care And Insurance." Health Affairs. Accessed February 5, 2019. https://www.healthaffairs.org/doi/full/10.1377/hlthaff.20.1.247.

26 Family HealthCare Network. "Our Story." Accessed February 7, 2019. https://www.fhcn.org/about/our-story-2/.

27 Neighbor's Link Pamphlet

28 Maine, Jillian. "The Importance of Patient Advocacy." *Nursing Critical Care* 10, no. 4 (July 2015): 48. doi: 10.1097/01.CCN.0000466773.16048.35.

29 National Cancer Institute. "NCI Dictionary of Cancer Terms." Accessed November 27, 2018. https://www.cancer.gov/publications/dictionaries/cancer-terms/def/patient-advocate.

30 Next Avenue. "The Importance of Hiring, or Being, a Patient Advocate." September 7, 2018. Accessed March 18, 2019. https://www.nextavenue.org/importance-patient-advocate/.

31 Clancy, Carolyn M., and Ahrq. "My Medical Manager: Why You May Need a Health Advocate." AARP. July 23, 2010. https://www.aarp.org/health/doctors-hospitals/info-07-2010/my_medical_manager_using_a_health_advocate.html.

32 Kaiser Family Foundation Analysis of the 2016 National Health Interview Survey

33 Migration Policy Institute. "2010 American Community Survey and census data on the foreign born by state." Accessed March 21, 2012. http://www.migrationinformation.org/datahub/acscensus.cfm.

34 Kaiser Commission on Medicaid and the Uninsured. "Summary of new health reform law; 2011." Accessed March 21, 2012. http://www.kff.org/healthreform/upload/8061.pdf.

35 Vargas Bustamante A, Chen J. "Health expenditure dynamics and years of US residence: analyzing spending disparities among Latinos by citizenship/nativity status." *Health Serv Res* 47, no.2 (2012):794-818.

36 Martinez, Omar, Elwin Wu, Theo Sandfort, et al. "Evaluating the impact of immigrant policies on health status among undocumented immigrants: a systematic review." *Journal of Immigrant and Minority Health* 17, vol. 3 (June 2015): 947–970. doi:10.1007/s10903-013-9968-4.

37 Mark Kuczewski, Johana Mejias-Beck and Amy Blair, "Good Sanctuary Doctoring for Undocumented Patients." *AMA Journal of Ethics* 21, no.1 (2019): E78-85. https://journalofethics.ama-assn.org/article/good-sanctuary-doctoring-undocumented-patients/2019-01.

38 Omolara T. Uwemedimo, Ana C. Monterrey, Julie M. Linton. "A Dream Deferred: Ending DACA Threatens Children, Families, and Communities." *Pediatrics* 140, no. 6 (December 2017): e20173089. doi:10.1542/peds.2017-3089

39 Vargas Bustamante A, Fang H, Garza J, et al. "Variations in healthcare access and utilization among Mexican immigrants: the role of documentation status." J Immigr Minor Health 14, no.1 (2012):146-155.

40 Bustamante, Arturo Vargas and Philip J. Van der Wees. "Integrating Immigrants into the US Health System." *American Medical Association Journal of Ethics* 14, no.4 (April 2012):318-323.